CLOTHES AND CRAFTS IN HISTORY

CLOTHES AND CRAFTS IN
VICTORIAN TIMES

Philip Steele

Gareth Stevens Publishing
A WORLD ALMANAC EDUCATION GROUP COMPANY

Gareth Stevens Publishing would like to thank Lance R. Grahn, Ph.D., Associate Professor of History, Marquette University, Milwaukee, Wisconsin, for his kind and professional help with the information in this book.

For a free color catalog describing Gareth Stevens' list of high-quality books and multimedia programs, call 1-800-542-2595 (USA) or 1-800-461-9120 (Canada). Gareth Stevens Publishing's Fax: (414) 332-3567.

Library of Congress Cataloging-in-Publication Data available upon request from publisher.
Fax: (414) 332-3567 for the attention of the Publishing Records Department.

ISBN 0-8368-2738-4

This edition first published in 2000 by
Gareth Stevens Publishing
A World Almanac Education Group Company
330 West Olive Street, Suite 100
Milwaukee, WI 53212 USA

Original © 1997 by Zoë Books Limited, Winchester, England.
Additional end matter © 2000 by Gareth Stevens, Inc.

Illustrations: Virginia Gray

Photographic acknowledgments

The publishers wish to acknowledge, with thanks, the following photographic sources:
Cover: e. t. archive/Private Collection, top right /Victoria & Albert Museum, London, center - Grandmother's Birthday by Josef Laurens Dyckmans, (1811-88); Ancient Art & Architecture Collection/Ellison, top left; © Michael Holford/Science Museum, London, bottom left; Mansell Collection, bottom right.

The American Museum in Britain, Bath 13t & b; Ancient Art & Architecture Collection 8t, 11tl, /Ellison 19b; The Bridgeman Art Library/Royal Holloway and Bedford New College, Surrey, title page - *The Railway Station*, 1862 by William Powell Frith (1819-1909) /Christie's Images, London 20 - *An Omnibus Ride to Piccadilly Circus, Mr. Gladstone Travelling with Ordinary Passengers* by Alfred Morgan, (fl. 1862-1904); C. M. Dixon/Victoria & Albert Museum, London 14b; e. t. archive 4t, 8b, 11tr, 14t, 15c, 22t, 25t /Private Collection 3 /Stoke Museum, Staffordshire 15t /Forrester 22bl /Wilkinson, National Library of Australia 23b /Musée de L'Ile de France 24t; Robert Harding Picture Library/Walter Rawlings/Victoria & Albert Museum, London 9t; © Michael Holford/Science Museum, London 6t, 7b /Bethnal Green Museum of Childhood, London 10 /American Museum, Bath, Gift of Mr. Frelinghuysen 12; Mansell Collection 4b, 5b, 6b, 11b, 16t & bl, 17b, 18t & b, 19t & c, 21t, 22br, 24b, 27tl; Philip Sauvain Picture Collection 5t, 7t, 16br, 17t, 21b, 25b /from *New York in the Nineteenth Century* by John Grafton, Dover Publications, Inc. 23t; Zefa 9b.

Printed in the United States of America

1 2 3 4 5 6 7 8 9 04 03 02 01 00

CONTENTS

Words that appear in the glossary are printed in
boldface type the first time they occur in the text.

INTRODUCTION

Between about 200 and 100 years ago, the way many people lived and worked changed a great deal. This period, the nineteenth century, is sometimes called the Victorian Age. It is named after Queen Victoria, who ruled Great Britain and Ireland from 1837 until 1901.

In the 1700s, most people in the British Isles lived in the peaceful countryside. But even then, new **factories** and mills were appearing among the green fields. Water wheels and steam power ran the **machines** inside the factories. New canals were built to carry goods such as pottery and **textiles** away from the factories.

In the 1800s, **industry** began to change the face of Britain. Richard Trevithick

◀ All kinds of inexpensive souvenirs were sold to mark the beginning of Victoria's reign in 1837. They included china plates, pitchers, cups, bottles, and small statues.

designed the world's first steam **locomotives** between 1802 and 1804, and soon new railroads stretched across the land. Ironworks and coal mines were built. Country people now poured into the big new cities to look for work.

◀ This map of the world was printed in 1886. New, **independent** nations were growing in the Americas at this time. Powerful European nations, such as Britain and France, were building the biggest **empires** the world had ever seen. The British Empire is colored pink on this map.

The empires provided cheap labor and **raw materials**, such as cotton, for the new factories. They also provided a **market** for goods.

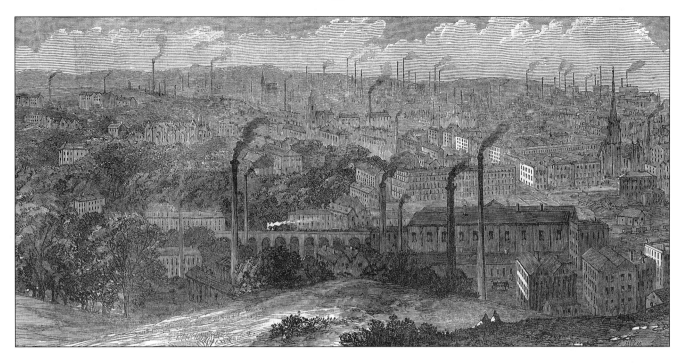

In the cities, housing was poor, wages were low, and even small children worked long hours to make profits for the factory owners. Tall chimneys coughed out smoke and soot.

This period became known as the Industrial Revolution. Many **craft** items that people had made by hand were now mass-produced in factories. The new ways of working spread from Britain to France, Belgium, Germany, and the growing cities in the eastern United States.

The Great Exhibition

In 1851, people from all over Britain visited London's Hyde Park to see a display of the world's crafts and **manufactured** goods. They marveled at all the new inventions. Prince Albert, Queen Victoria's husband, organized this Great Exhibition. It took place inside an enormous glass building called the Crystal Palace.

▲ Factory chimneys stretch as far as the eye can see at Halifax, England, in 1882. Many of these factories were producing cloth.

▼ The Crystal Palace was specially built for the Great Exhibition. Its parts were first made, and then put together on site. It was the world's first **prefabricated** building. Later it was moved from Hyde Park to South London.

VICTORIAN CRAFTS

Handcrafts or machines?

For thousands of years people produced crafts by hand. Some goods were made at home, and others in small workshops. The makers either used the crafts themselves or sold them at local markets. Some goods were sold abroad, or **exported**, but transportation was slow. However, by the beginning of the 1800s, times were changing.

People were making new scientific discoveries and inventions. This meant that new **technologies** were being developed. In Victorian factories there were clanking water wheels, hissing steam engines, and crashing steam hammers.

▼ People wove cloth by hand, on frames called looms, for thousands of years. But by the 1830s, steam-powered machine looms, like these, were widespread.

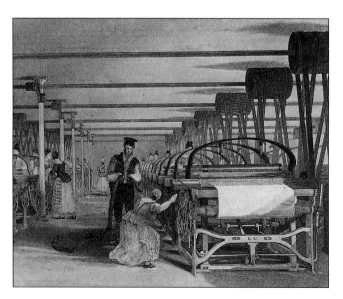

▲ Instead of using plants and earth to make dyes for textiles, people began to use chemicals. New **synthetic dyes** with brilliant colors were invented in 1856. These two were called mauveine and alizarin.

In the **potteries**, steam-powered machines mixed clays and shaped and **molded** plates and pitchers. Decorations were put on, using transfers. In the leather industry, machines ground up tree bark and pumped water for treating, or tanning, the leather. Other machines stitched the finished leather.

New gas-fired **furnaces** were used in glass making. Glass was now made in large sheets. Important changes also happened in the metal industries, where new furnaces produced higher quality iron. Henry Bessemer, an Englishman, and William Siemens, a German, invented

▲ These **cutlers** are making knives in the English town of Sheffield. Sheffield was a world center of steel production. The picture comes from a magazine published in 1884.

Inventions of the 1800s

1800	Iron printing press, England
1801	Jacquard loom, France
1821	Electric motor, England
1822	Photography, France
1823	Waterproof clothing, Scotland
1830	Sewing machine, France
1832	Pixii's dynamo, France
1839	Steam hammer, England
1856	Bessemer steel, England
	Synthetic dyes, England
1862	First plastic, England
1877	Phonograph, U.S.
1884	Steam turbine, England
	Artificial fiber, France
1891	Zip fastener, U.S.
1893	Fiberglass, U.S.

better ways of making steel between 1856 and 1866.

However, all these changes did take time. Some handcrafts continued side by side with the new machine crafts. Many manufacturing industries were only partly **mechanized**. Even in a factory, people made parts, or fittings, for the machines using traditional craft skills.

The new machinery put many handcraft workers out of business. In 1811, stocking makers from Nottingham, in England, smashed new knitting and lace-making machines. These rioters were called "Luddites," after Ned Ludd, who had destroyed machinery in Leicestershire about 30 years before. "Luddite" riots lasted until 1816.

▶ This sewing machine, made in 1869, was for use in hot, wet countries. It has a special plating to protect it from rust.

Arts and crafts

From the earliest times, people have enjoyed producing beautiful objects. Many Victorians began to realize that although factories could mass-produce items cheaply, the goods were often poor in design and quality.

Many people in Europe became interested in high-quality hand crafts. An English writer called William Morris (1834-96) and his friends set up an arts and crafts movement to bring back the traditional craft skills. Their workshops and factories produced beautiful glass, tiles, pottery, carpets, wallpapers, textiles and furniture.

William Morris was interested in new political ideas such as socialism. He was shocked by working conditions in the new factories and towns. He wanted workers to be paid fairly and to be treated with respect.

▲ A detail from *The Orchard* tapestry, designed by William Morris in 1890.

◀ M.H. Baillie Scott, a member of the Arts and Crafts movement, designed this dining room in 1901.

▲ This is William Morris's design, *The Strawberry Thief*. It was printed on cotton material called chintz.

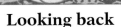

Looking back

In the early 1800s, European craft designers were inspired by the **classical** styles of ancient Rome. During Queen Victoria's reign, designers looked back to the European Middle Ages. Rich nobles built and furnished houses that looked like castles, copying a **medieval** style called Gothic.

Mass production was here to stay, but William Morris's ideas did influence other people. The tradition of fine craft work continued through the late 1890s and into the next century. The work of young Scottish architect Charles Rennie Mackintosh (1868-1928) and his wife, the designer Margaret Macdonald Mackintosh, was admired throughout Europe. They were influenced by styles known in French as *Art Nouveau* ("new art") and in German as *Jugendstil* ("youth style").

▶ This fairy-tale castle is at Neuschwanstein, Germany. It looks like a medieval castle, but it is only about 125 years old. The castle was built for the mad King of Bavaria, Ludwig II.

"Cozy clutter"

What were Victorian homes like? There were big differences between the social classes. Nobles and the rich lived in huge mansions and were waited on by many servants. Middle-class people kept servants, too, and lived in roomy houses. Poor people had few belongings. They lived in small country cottages or in city **tenements** without running water.

Victorians who could afford it lived in comfort. They liked overstuffed armchairs and patterned carpets. Screens and heavy curtains kept out the drafts. Their furniture was grand. It was often made of hardwoods such as **mahogany**.

▼ Dollhouses were popular with Victorian children. This one is beautifully made. It shows many of the rooms in a big Victorian house. There are servants' quarters and a children's nursery.

▲ This engraving by Cruikshank makes fun of families who bought objects just for decoration. The poker is made of soft metal, which will melt if it is used to stir the fire.

▶ This book was printed in 1879. The gold decoration on the book cover was made by hand. The Victorians liked to display highly decorated books in their homes.

Victorian rooms were cluttered with objects, some handcrafted and others manufactured. There were ornaments and potted plants, such as aspidistras, and stuffed animals and birds in glass cases. **Parlors** usually contained a glass-fronted cabinet for displaying china. Heating came either from open fires or from iron stoves or **ranges**. Over the fireplaces mantelpieces were ornate. They were made from polished stone such as marble, **serpentine**, or slate.

There were fine bookcases in many homes. Changes in printing meant that it was now cheaper to produce large numbers of books and magazines, and cheaper to buy them. More people received some education in the 1800s than in the 1700s.

▼ All kinds of tableware are displayed in this shop.

Shopping for crafts

In Victorian Paris, London, and New York, large department stores opened. They sold everything from clothes to furniture and china. Some stores sold cheap, mass-produced items. Others sold expensive handcrafts. Liberty's in London had fine craft work especially made for their shop.

Homemade

People still made crafts in the home or on a small, local basis. This happened in country cottages and farms all over Europe and in the lands where the **pioneers** were settling in the United States, Canada, and Australia.

These craft items were often simple but beautiful, made according to regional styles and traditions. They included woolen shawls and stockings, delicate lace and finely stitched embroidery, baskets made of rush or willow, mats made of grasses or rags, furniture, woodcarvings, and pottery.

▲ This beautiful patchwork quilt was made in the United States around the 1840s. Bedcovers like this were made from scraps of material. Sometimes several women met to join sections of patchwork and attach the backing fabric and the soft filling.

Some crafts were traditionally made by women, and others by men. The skills and often the tools of the trade were passed down from mother to daughter and from father to son.

Victorian city dwellers developed a **sentimental** love of the countryside. Soon factories were producing furniture in styles known as "cottage" or "**rustic**." These styles had little to do with the real country crafts.

Crafts such as needlework and embroidery were considered "ladylike" for girls and women in middle- and upper-class homes. They spent long hours sewing.

▲ Samplers are pieces of cloth that show skills in needlework. In Victorian times young girls in most parts of Europe and North America made samplers. They stitched letters of the alphabet, family names, verses from the Bible, pictures, and mottos.

The Shakers

The Shakers were a group of religious people who moved to North America from England in 1774. They gained many followers during the 1800s. They lived very simple lives, farming and making their own linen and leather. Their most famous craft was furniture making. Shaker furniture is admired for its beauty and simplicity. The photograph (below) shows a reconstruction of a Shaker living room.

Eastern influences

The Great Exhibition, held in London in 1851, included traditional craft items from all over the world. Some of the finest crafts of the nineteenth century came from Asia and Africa.

▲ This gold chest was made in India. It contains perfume bottles and jewelry made of gold and decorated with precious stones.

▼ This detail of a dragon was embroidered in silk. It is from a robe belonging to the Chinese Emperor, which was made in the 1850s.

China and Japan were centers of **porcelain** manufacture. Some of the goods, such as plates and vases, were made for the Western market. They were sometimes less beautiful than the local designs.

The porcelain factory at Seto in Japan produced china for the European market in the 1800s. Blue and white porcelain and huge decorated vases were very popular.

◀ This richly colored dish was made around 1890 by William de Morgan.

▼ This is a drawing of a fine cabinet that was made by the Victorian craftsman E.W. Godwin. He was inspired by traditional Japanese designs.

Crafts from Asia were particularly popular in the West. Travelers brought back some items as personal souvenirs, and traders **imported** other crafts.

Designers in the Arts and Crafts Movement began to look eastward to Japan for ideas. Japanese furniture was simple, beautiful, and cleverly constructed.

Between the 1870s and 1890s chinoiserie was a popular fashion in Europe and the United States. This style of furniture and furnishings imitated Far Eastern styles. Sitting rooms were full of Chinese lanterns, bamboo tables, and **rattan** or wickerwork chairs. Folding screens coated with varnish kept out drafts.

The beautiful people

During the 1880s and 1890s, the Aesthetic Movement grew up in Europe and North America. "Aesthetics" means the study of beauty. People thought that poetry and art were very important. Persian rugs, Indian shawls, and *Art Nouveau* items became very popular. Magazines such as the London *Punch* made fun of the Aesthetic Movement.

CLOTHES AND FASHION

Paris fashions

Paris, the capital of France, was the center of world fashion. From Moscow to New York, people studied pictures in fashion magazines. The latest Parisian styles of clothes, hats, hair fashions, and jewelry were widely copied.

Napoleon I, who was crowned emperor of France in 1804, gave great support to the French textile industry. The latest looms,

◄ An "Empire" line dress, around 1810

invented in England, were ordered for factories at Sedan and Louviers. Saint-Quentin was famous at this time for **muslin** and linen. Valenciennes produced fine lace and a thin satin called tulle.

Napoleon even ordered that no lady should appear at the French court wearing the same dress twice! To wear the Paris fashions, women needed to be rich and to lead a life of leisure. Many designs were very impractical and uncomfortable. They were not suitable for work or other activity.

▼ A ball dress made of pink silk with a white-flowered gauze overdress, from the 1850s

▲ 1830s evening dresses

The "Empire" line, which was popular about 1810, was probably the most comfortable women's fashion of the 1800s. It was inspired by ancient Greek and Roman tunics, or chemises. Dresses and coats were high-waisted with loose skirts. The style was worn with sashes and shawls. By the 1830s, dresses had wide skirts and puffed sleeves with frills, pleats, and bows. In about 1855, fashionable women wore a **crinoline**. This dress had a huge, bell-shaped skirt over hoops of steel and **whalebone**. Beneath it women wore layers of stiff underskirts and long lace pantaloons.

By about 1875 the crinoline had gone out of fashion. Skirts were now swept up at the back into a padded cushion called a bustle. At the front the skirt material clung tightly around the knees.

▲ An advertisement for ladies' corsets

Corset madness

Many Victorian women laced themselves tightly into whalebone **corsets**, for the "wasp-waisted" look. These corsets squeezed the insides of their bodies. Some women's dresses had waists of 22 inches (56 cm) or less!

◀ Afternoon dresses with bustles and bows, the fashion in 1878

Fashion accessories

There was more to being fashionable than wearing the right dress. Women's hairstyles varied over the years from tight ringlets and buns to loops and coils of plaits. In the early 1800s fashionable ladies wore **turbans**. These were later replaced by bonnets and lace caps. At the end of the century, hats decorated with feathers or flowers were fashionable.

No respectable woman used much, if any, face makeup in the Victorian period.

▲ A fashionable turban in 1810

Shoe fashions varied through the century, from light slippers to elegant buttoned boots.

In winter rich women wore fur capes, hats, and muffs. In warm weather they carried a sunshade or parasol. They also used fans to keep themselves cool. Parasols, fans, and handbags were usually beautifully made. They were used as fashion items as much as for practical purposes.

Jewelry was very popular. Women wore earrings, rings,

◄ Some hairstyles used false hairpieces and pads. Women wore bows, flowers, and jewels in their hair at parties.

These are morning and evening dresses, the "latest" fashions in 1833.

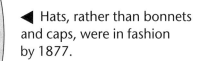

▲ In Victorian times lace was used for handkerchiefs, veils, caps, collars, and dress and underwear trimmings.

bracelets, and necklaces. Wealthy ladies wore jewels and **tiaras** in their hair at grand balls. In the 1890s, tight necklaces, or "chokers," were fashionable. They were made of jeweled ribbons, strings of pearls, or **jet**. Gold or silver chains held lockets, which were small cases containing pictures of loved ones.

◀ Hats, rather than bonnets and caps, were in fashion by 1877.

▼ A silver pocket watch made in Geneva, Switzerland, in the 1800s

Plumes and feathers

The fashion industry used huge numbers of feathers, mainly to decorate hats. In the 1850s, ostrich plumes were very popular. Ostrich farms were set up in Cape Province, South Africa, to supply the trade. However, hunting threatened many kinds of wild birds that had spectacular feathers. By the 1890s about 50,000 birds of paradise were exported from the forests of New Guinea every year.

Men and children

In the early 1800s, men still wore knee-length breeches and stockings, as they had done in the 1700s. However, tight-fitting trousers then became fashionable. By Victoria's reign, looser trousers were worn.

Victorian men wore long woolen underwear, and sometimes corsets to keep their stomachs in! Shirts had separate collars, stiffened with starch and attached with studs. Men always wore a waistcoat. Evening waistcoats were made of silk, satin, or velvet. Neckties were folded like **cravats** or tied in bows.

▲ William Gladstone, Prime Minister of Great Britain in the late 1800s, is wearing a silk top hat in this painting, *An Omnibus Ride to Piccadilly Circus.*

Men's coats were tight-fitting, with a heavy collar and long tails. At the start of the century, men wore brighter colors, but darker shades later became fashionable. Most respectable businessmen wore black. In 1823 a Scotsman called Charles Macintosh discovered how to use rubber and turpentine to make cloth waterproof. He had invented the raincoat.

Men's wigs went out of fashion in Victorian times. Men began to wear their

▲ In this photograph Prince Albert has fashionable side whiskers and a mustache. Notice how his striped waistcoat matches Queen Victoria's dress.

hair longer, and side whiskers, beards, and mustaches became popular. The silk top hat arrived, and remained in fashion into the 1900s. In the 1860s a round, stiff hat

The dandies

In Britain, 1811-1820 was known as the **Regency** period. Prince George ruled in place of his father, George III, who was ill. Some of the prince's friends, led by "Beau" Brummell, created high fashion styles for men. These wearers of extreme fashions were called "dandies."

made of felt appeared. It was named after a London hatter called John Bowler.

Men wore tall boots for riding and traveling and light shoes or slippers at other times. They sometimes buttoned cloth or leather **gaiters** over their shoes.

Very small children of both sexes wore skirted tunics. When crinolines were still fashionable, older girls wore shorter, full-skirted dresses, which showed the bottoms of their lace-trimmed pantaloons. Around the 1900s boys and girls were often dressed in sailor suits. School children wore pinafores to protect their clothes.

A velvet sailor suit

A boy's tweed suit

◀ In the Victorian period, men had to make sure that their clothes were exactly right for every social occasion. They paid close attention to detail and style.

The man on the far left wears a formal frock coat and a top hat. The man next to him is wearing a tweed suit and a bowler hat.

Working dress

During the nineteenth century, soldiers wore some of the fanciest costumes. The troops of most countries wore splendid uniforms in scarlet, blue, green, or white. They had gold braid, **epaulettes**, and plumed headgear.

Victorian firefighters wore splendid uniforms, too, with shiny helmets. The first police in Britain wore top hats and dark suits. Later they wore helmets. Clergymen, teachers, and university lecturers all wore their

From scarlet to khaki

In the 1850s, British troops were fighting in India. They wore uniforms in a brown color called khaki, which were harder for the enemy to see. By the end of the century, colorful uniforms were beginning to disappear from battlefields.

own kinds of uniforms, such as black gowns and flat-topped caps called mortarboards.

Servants in rich households wore a uniform, or livery, in the family colors. Menservants often dressed in the style of the 1700s, with breeches, stockings, and powdered wigs.

▲ A gunner from the British Royal Horse Artillery, around 1815

◄ The women who carried water in the French army were called *cantinières*. In 1860 they wore this uniform.

▶ In the middle-class homes of the 1880s and 1890s, cooks and parlor maids wore mob caps, aprons, and long dresses.

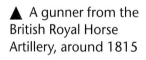

Working people wore rough, strong clothes in heavy cloth or **corduroy**. In Britain, farm workers wore linen smocks and neckerchiefs. Working men and women wore boots or wooden clogs.

The cowboys of the North American West wore boots, broad-brimmed hats, and leather leggings, or chaps.

In the cities of Europe and the eastern United States, poor people could not even begin to think about fashion. Many wore patched and ragged second-hand clothes, and their children went without shoes.

▶ Many people lived and worked in the poor areas, or slums, of big cities. Churches and charities provided them with some clothing and food. This drawing shows women and children at work on the streets of New York in 1890.

◀ These miners came to Ballarat, Australia, in the 1850s to search for gold. In Australia, Canada, and the United States, pioneers wore heavy coats, tough boots, and wide-brimmed hats.

Dressing for leisure

In the later Victorian period, people began to be interested in sports, athletics, and outdoor pursuits such as rock-climbing and rowing.

At first, people wore their ordinary clothes to play new sports such as "Sphairistiké" (lawn tennis). Stiff Victorian clothing was possible for sports such as croquet or archery, but not for more active sports–when even a glimpse of a lady's ankle was rather shocking!

Men wore vests and long shorts for sports such as soccer, but such dress was not respectable for sportswomen. Some women wanted easier ways of dressing. Amelia Bloomer (1818-94), an American, designed and wore baggy breeches, which

▲ This woman cyclist of 1895 is wearing bloomers. She was making a daring move toward more practical clothes for women.

▼ Boat trips were popular at the end of the nineteenth century. Both men and women wore straw hats called boaters. These hats were still fashionable in the 1920s.

◀ French fashions for sporting costumes for men and women, 1880

were called bloomers after her. These shocked many people, but they were ideal for cycling, the latest popular activity for women.

The upper classes and many country people loved hunting. Those who could afford it wore formal dress for hunting. It included red or green men's jackets, top hats or caps, and special jackets and skirts, called riding habits, for women.

Bathing belles

The fashion for swimming in the ocean began in the Regency Period. By the end of the century, the railroads carried thousands of ordinary families to the beaches for vacations. Women wore frilly bathing dresses and caps, and men wore long woolen costumes.

▶ As swimming in the ocean became more popular, Victorians became less worried about public modesty. But they still changed for swimming in wheeled beach huts, called bathing machines.

FESTIVALS AND HOLIDAYS

Victorians are often remembered for their seriousness and respectability rather than for their sense of fun. Queen Victoria once wrote "We are not amused"–and this has been seen as the spirit of her times. However, most people did know how to enjoy themselves. All across Europe there were seasonal local fairs. People put on their best clothes for a fair. The streets were full of entertainers, pie sellers, and peddlers selling ribbons, buttons, and simple crafts.

Harvest was celebrated with a supper, often held in a barn, to which everyone who had helped was invited. In North America, too, farmers gathered for barn dances and local fairs.

Rich people celebrated birthdays and public events with glittering balls and gave each other gifts of jewels.

It was the Victorians who began to celebrate the Christmas festival as we know it. The German custom of candle-lit Christmas trees spread across Europe and North America. The Victorians also started the habit of sending greeting cards to their families at Christmas and to their sweethearts on Valentine's Day.

A Russian Easter egg

In 1884 the ruler of Russia, Czar Alexander III, commissioned the famous goldsmith Peter Carl Fabergé to make a jeweled "Easter egg" as a present for his wife. It was the first of many. You can make a special egg for Easter, too, even if you don't have real jewels.

You will need: • one hen's egg • pin • bowl • pencil • paints • glitter • foil • scissors • glue.

1. Take a hen's egg and make a hole in each end with a pin.

2. Hold the egg over the bowl. Blow into one hole until all the egg inside has come out of the other hole.

3. Draw a pattern on the eggshell with your pencil.

4. Paint the pattern in red, purple, and gold.

5. Decorate with glitter.

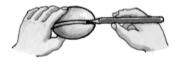

6. Cut out small diamond shapes of foil and glue them onto the shell.

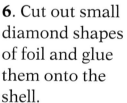

A Victorian valentine

Valentine's Day (February 14) is the day to declare your love. Design a card in the Victorian style.

You will need: • poster paper • scissors • pencil • colored pencils • pen • perhaps some pressed flowers and glue.

1. Use the scissors to cut out a rectangle of paper the size you want. Fold it in half.

2. Draw a heart shape on the front flap and cut it out. Trace the shape through the cut onto the inside flap. Color it in.

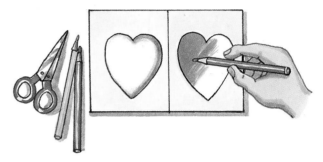

3. Decorate the front with drawings of violets and roses, copied from a book. Or you may like to try pressing a winter flower between the pages of a book and gluing this onto the card.

4. Make up a small poem to write inside the card, the more sentimental the better.

5. Give it to your sweetheart, if you dare!

A silhouette of Victoria

Silhouettes were popular in Victorian times. They are portraits in which the outline of the person's head or body is filled in with plain black. They look like a shadow, or like somebody standing against the sunlight.

You will need: • black construction paper • scissors • tracing paper • pencil • chalk • stiff white paper • paste.

1. This picture shows Queen Victoria, aged 18. Use a pencil to copy the outline of the head onto the tracing paper.

2. Rub the other side of the tracing paper with white chalk and place it on top of the black paper. Trace the outline.

3. Cut out the shape of the head from the black paper.

4. Paste it onto the white paper as backing.

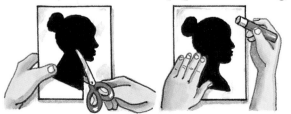

Découpage

On a rainy day, Victorian children might cut pictures from magazines and advertisements and paste them into a scrapbook or onto screens and boxes. This process, called découpage, made attractive designs and patterns.

You will need: • scissors • paste • plain cardboard gift box • old magazines.

1. Cut out all sorts of objects from pictures in the magazines.

2. Group them together according to subject, color, or shape.

3. Lay some of them out on the top of the box. Make sure they fit closely together to make patterns. Glue them in position.

4. Turn the box on to its side. Fit more pictures together and glue them in position. Repeat this on each side of the box, until it is covered with pictures.

Punch and Judy

Victorian children loved seaside Punch and Judy shows. Make your own Punch and Judy puppets and put on a show.

You will need: • poster paper • pencil • tracing paper • scissors • colored felt pens • glue • Popsicle sticks.

1. Trace the patterns below onto the poster paper and cut them out.

2. Color them in.

3. Paste them onto the sticks, and you have your puppets.

GLOSSARY

classical: Relating to ancient Greece or ancient Rome.

corduroy: A thick, ridged cotton cloth.

corset: A tight-laced garment to make a waist look smaller.

crafts: Trades or pastimes in which people use skills to make things by hand.

cravat: A broad cloth folded and tied around the neck.

crinoline: A full-skirted dress supported by hoops.

cutler: A maker of knives, forks, and spoons.

empire: A group of countries ruled by one government.

epaulette: A fringed shoulder decoration on military uniforms.

export: To send goods to another country for sale.

factory: A building used for manufacturing goods.

furnace: A very hot oven used in industry.

gaiter: A leg-covering, buttoned over footwear.

import: To bring goods from another country to sell.

independent: Free from the rule of another country.

industry: Work, trade, or manufacture.

jet: A shiny black stone used in making jewelry.

locomotive: An engine that pulls a train.

machines: Engines or tools that do work for people.

mahogany: A very hard wood cut from tropical forests.

manufactured: Made by an industrial process.

market: (1) A place where goods are bought and sold.
(2) A group of people who buy certain goods.

mechanized: Using machinery.

medieval: The period between about A.D. 500 and 1500, also known as the Middle Ages.

mold: To shape an object using a hollow form.

muslin: A very fine, gauzy cotton cloth.

parlor: A sitting room, living room, or reception room.

pioneers: People who are among the first to do something.

porcelain: Thin china of the highest quality.

potteries:	Workshops or factories producing pottery.
prefabricated:	Made in advance somewhere else and then put together on site.
range:	A built-in iron stove used for heating or cooking.
rattan:	Stem of an Asian palm, used in making furniture.
raw material:	Any natural material, such as cotton or iron ore, used in the manufacture of goods.
regency:	The time during which another person rules on behalf of a king or queen who is too young or too ill to rule.
rustic:	In a country style, simply or roughly made.
sentimental:	Appealing to feelings and emotions.
serpentine:	A polished stone, often reddish or greenish in color.
synthetic dye:	A manufactured chemical used for coloring.
technology:	The use of scientific ideas in industrial processes.
tenement:	A building divided into many separate dwellings.
textile:	A cloth made by weaving.
tiara:	A crown-like head ornament, worn by women.
turban:	A hat made by winding cloth around the head.
whalebone:	A bendable plastic-like substance from the jaws of a baleen whale. It was used to stiffen corsets.

FURTHER READING

Costumes and Clothes. Legacies (series). Penelope Paul (Thomson Learning)

Daily Life in a Victorian House. Laura Wilson (Puffin)

High Fashion in Victorian Times: A Study of Period Costume With Pull-Up Scenes. Andrew Brownfoot (Parkwest)

Queen Victoria. British History Maker (series). Leon Ashworth (Cherrytree Books)

Queen Victoria. First Book (series). Robert Green (Franklin Watts)

Victorian Christmas. Bobbie Kalman (Crabtree)

Victorian Days: Discover the Past with Fun Projects, Games, Activities, and Recipes. David C. King (John Wiley & Sons)

Victorian Toys and Games. Victorian Life (series). Katrina Siliprandi (Wayland)

INDEX